W

"Your devotions have had a wonderful impact on my life. Today I accepted the Lord Jesus as my personal savior. Feels pretty good! I have a lot to learn about Jesus and the Bible, and your devotionals are a quick and easy way to do just that."
Danielle Kennedy

"Being always on the go and on business travel, your devotions have helped me focus on God in the middle of all this worldliness." *Financial Analyst, NC*

"Your devotions always have a direct impact on what is going on with my life everyday." *Congressional Aide*

"My husband lost his job this week but our faith has been encouraged by leaps and bounds thanks to your devotions." *Day Care Mom, CA*

"It is hard to find daily devotionals that focus more on scripture than on the author's opinion's. Dr. Hoy has done an excellent job." *Congressional Aide, CO*

"A source of spiritual refreshment in my ministry to US and NATO soldiers." *Active Duty Chaplain stationed in Bosnia and Herzegovina*

"Practical and essential to living! Not watered down and no compromising. The Word of God taken to a level of clarity for the current day." *H. Goodman*

"Exactly what I need to hear at the exact time I need to hear it!" *Professor, VA*

Words of Faith

Faith that Works

45 Days to a Deeper Walk With God

Dr. Jeffrey D. Hoy

First Edition

Halyard Press, Inc.
Melbourne, Florida

Published by:
Halyard Press, Inc.
P.O. Box 410308
Melbourne, FL 32941-0308
800-791-21111; Fax (407) 636-5370

Printed in the United States of America 1997

ISBN 1-887063-05-6

Dedication

To my Lord, and Savior Jesus;

His gift to me, my precious wife, Ann;

and my blessings from heaven:

Tiffany, Jeffrey and Andrew.

Contents

Lay Foundations

"...a servant of God and of the Lord Jesus Christ."
James 1:1

Gain Perspective

"...in humble circumstances take pride in the high position."
James 1:9

Make Priorities

"... the crown of life that God has promised."
James 1:12

Refine Essentials

"...humbly accept the word planted in you, which can save you."
James 1:21

Restore Relationship

"...faith by itself, if it is not accompanied by action, is dead."
James 2:17

Walk It

"...his faith was made complete by what he did."
James 2:22

Talk It

"...if anyone is never at fault in what he says, he is a perfect man."
James 3:2

Live It

"...humble yourselves before the Lord, and He will lift you up."
James 4:10

Love It

"...be patient and stand firm, because the Lord's coming is near."
James 5:8

Preface

I encourage you to encounter God in His Word as you consider the thoughts on these pages. This book was originally written in an E-mail version to encourage busy Christian believers who spend a part of their day in front of a computer. Now, this print form extends a devotional encounter beyond the computer.

I extend my special thanks and gratitude to the wonderful people of Faith Fellowship Church who have allowed me the privilege of serving as their Pastor Teacher. I also extend gratitude to the thousands of people who allow me to share with them thoughts about God's Word through the Words of Faith Daily E-mail Devotional. I owe a great debt of gratitude to Sandy Merritt who prepared the manuscript for publication and Dick Blondin for the cover design. Also to my favorite English teacher, Donna Sue Armstrong (my mother) for careful proof reading and my beloved Ann for proof reading and for encouraging me to write.

Jeff Hoy
Faith Fellowship Church
Melbourne, Florida
August 1997

Introduction

We live in an age when many voices speak of spirituality. This book is designed as a reflective tool to aid you in sorting out those voices as you develop a deeper walk with God. To get to that deeper walk of faith, we will dig deeply into one of the most challenging and practical books in the Bible—the Letter of James. This short book is often framed as a debate between faith and works, but I believe that within this brief and powerful letter to all Christians we will discover a Faith that Works. The wisdom and clear practicality of James spoke to believers in the first century and continues to lift us as we near the end of the second millennium. Here you will find practical, real life faith in action without the cliches or easy answers that often come up empty.

The forty-five brief reflections in this book have been divided into nine sections. You may want to commit to daily reading for a nine week period as you seek a deepening of your walk with God. You may want to study in a small group or class as you reflect weekly on the challenges of God's Word. Faith that Works can also be used as a seasonal study for Advent or Lent. My only suggestion is this—Don't rush. The power of James is in allowing the Word to penetrate—soak in—challenge and reform us.

So let's get started! Can you imagine what it was like to grow up as the brother of Jesus? Actually growing up with the Word made flesh? And you think you had a perfect sibling to compete with? While we might imagine that it was difficult growing up with a "perfect older brother," we can also be sure that Jesus lived his message at home.

God gives us a wonderful gift through this brother
of our Lord.   James can give us a unique perspective on Jesus.   James the brother of Jesus probably
came to faith after a healthy dose of skepticism.
He then carried the church as a leader through
some of the most difficult of times. James had to
deal with harsh realities that came with persecution
and poverty—jealousy and church strife. He wrote
some of the most powerful and practical words we
find in the New Testament as well as some of the
oldest recorded. James encouraged a broad
audience of Christian believers scattered across the
world as they faced difficult times and issues. So
shall he encourage us.

Church strife — struggling

Identity

James 1:1

James, a servant of God and of the Lord Jesus Christ...

I will never forget the first youth group that I served as a student. When my wife and I met the seven youth who came that first night, we went around the room to introduce ourselves. One precious little eighth grader told us only her first name. I didn't think much about it until later when we asked what her last name was. She confided a bit sheepishly that she did not know. She went on to explain that because of a complicated divorce and custody situation in her family that was not resolved, she was called one name at school and another at home. She was not sure who she was at church.

The truth is that many of us arrive at church, or wherever we go, in much the same state. We come wondering who we are. We come in search of identity. We ask—*Who am I? Where did I come from? Where am I going? What am I called in this place?* Our confusion may not be as literally profound as the young lady in the youth group, but all of us begin our journey of faith with this sort of self discovery. In that searching we discover that we are created by God. We are in need of His grace. In Him we are righteous and in Him we find peace.

James is helpful in this search. For James, identity was no mystery. James begins his letter to Christians of every generation with these simple words of identity: "James, a servant of God and of the Lord Jesus Christ..." These words could sound deeply religious except when we consider they were written by the brother of Jesus. Can you imagine the humility involved for James? He was very likely among the family members who initially felt that Jesus had lost His mind. But now he affirms that Jesus is Lord. That is surrender.

The truth is that the Christian journey begins at a point of surrender. Perhaps we can remember a time when we thought that following Jesus was crazy or fanatical or worse. But at some point we surrender to that which seems crazy. "Love so amazing... so divine... demands my life my soul my all..." *Surrender* may be one of the most important words in our Christian language. Without it— we cannot even begin. Are you surrendered? Are you a servant of God? For James, that meant being available no matter what.

Lord, make me a servant. I surrender to Your will and Your way in my life. Have thine own way, Lord. Have thine own way. Amen.

Scattered

James 1:1

To the twelve tribes scattered among the nations...

James wrote with a Jewish heart. For centuries the Jewish people had been scattered across the Mediterranean world by the various political pressures of the day. While there was always a longing for the gathering of the people of God in Jerusalem, the identity of Judaism became very much that of a scattered people.

This is part of our Christian identity as well. Though we have been gathered in spirit by the work of Christ—we are scattered among the nations. Even Pentecost had the powerful act of gathering people in the power of the Holy Spirit and then scattering them to seventeen different places. It is no wonder that Jesus used the image of salt to describe the people of God. We are the salt of the earth—a scattering among the "nations"—intended to flavor and heighten the sensitivity of people to the working of God's spirit in their place. Because of that, our individual place is unique. Our points of influence are significant. For those James addressed, persecution had made this scattered life even more difficult. But James will call us to "count it joy" even in these scattered places of trial.

Where are you today? Are you scattered? Feeling a bit far from the shaker? God has something special He wants you to do exactly where you are.

Lord, thank You for the places You shall scatter me this day. Let me be salt and light in a lost world. Let me bring the flavor of Your Spirit to the places I visit and to the home where I dwell. In Jesus' name. Amen.

Joy

James 1:2

*Consider it pure joy, my brothers, whenever you
face trials of many kinds...*

When you press an orange, what comes out?
Orange juice, of course. When you press a person—what comes out? Well, that depends, doesn't
it? James says we should look for joy to come out
in the pressure points of life.   Frankly, it is one of
the most difficult admonitions in the Bible—How
can we count it joy when things are difficult? It
makes no sense. How can a smile attend a trial?
How can we rejoice in the difficult times of life?

The only way is to realize that James is calling
us to a different definition of Joy—Biblical Joy.
First of all—Biblical Joy is not something based
upon our circumstances. It is not something based
upon people or things. Biblical Joy does not find its
source in anything earthly and therefore cannot be
dissuaded by any condition that is earthly.

But more importantly, Biblical Joy is named
as a fruit of God's Spirit in us (Galatians 5:22 ff.).
It does not really depend upon us. And in many
ways, Joy is more like a "Juice of the Spirit." Joy is
that which flows out of us under pressure when we
are indwelled and empowered by the Spirit.
Instead of being the least likely response when the
pressure is on—it is the most likely. Joy is not
"happiness"—it is not some contrived silliness—or
a put-on smile. Joy is a deep and abiding peace

that rests and rejoices in God—no matter what.

Lord, Give me Your Joy today—no matter what. No matter the pressure—may Your fruit of Joy flow out of me under the squeeze. May the Joy of the Lord be my strength. In Jesus' name.

Testing

James 1:3

*...because you know that the testing of your faith
develops perseverance.*

Do you remember the story of Biosphere 2? A number of scientists sequestered themselves in a self-sustaining environment for two years. They studied a number of mini environments including an ocean, a desert and a rain forest, as well as various weather conditions. The only thing they could not study was wind. The interesting effect was that in the windless environment, the acacia trees planted in the Biosphere bent over and snapped. It seems that without the pressure of the wind to strengthen the wood, the trunks became too weak and could not hold up their own weight.

James suggests that the same thing is true with our faith. It is the pressure of testing that strengthens our faith so that it can hold us up. Without the testing of our faith, we would snap even under our own weight of living. God allows the wind to strengthen the acacia tree. God allows testing to make us strong.

Have you ever watched the tempering of steel? It is a process by which the steel is heated and then cooled—heated and then cooled. Fired red hot and then plunged into oil. It is an even more deliberate process than the testing of the acacia tree. But the truth is that our faith becomes strong only when it is tempered and tested.

Heated and then anointed. God allows us to be heated—never to the point of melting—but then we are plunged into the cooling oil of His love and Holy Spirit. As we are heated and then anointed, we slowly gain the powerful faith that will be needed as we serve Him.

I don't know about you, but I have sometimes prayed: " Lord, whatever it is You are trying to teach me—show me quick! Whatever tempering is needed—could we get done with it!?" But there are no shortcuts. No "faith pills" to pop. Sometimes the trials seem to go on and on, but with each heating—and each anointing—with each gust of the wind of His Spirit against our trunk of faith— we are formed more and more into the likeness of Christ with a faith that will stand.

Lord, strengthen me with the winds of Your Spirit. Temper me with the heat of living for You. Test the metal of my faith as You test the mettle of my soul that I may be strengthened for every task You have for me. In Jesus' name. Amen.

Perseverance

James 1:4

Perseverance must finish its work so that you may be mature and complete, not lacking anything.

There are many qualities of God that we seek: Love, joy, peace, mercy. What about perseverance? If anything can be said of the character of God, it is that He perseveres. God finishes what He starts. God works through the hard times. God perseveres because He is the God of completion—not lacking anything. We persevere differently—so that we may *become* mature and complete, not lacking anything. Through perseverance, we become who and what God wants us to be. We have Character. Paul put it this way: *Not only so, but we also rejoice in our sufferings, because we know that suffering produces perseverance; perseverance, character; and character, hope. And hope does not disappoint us, because God has poured out his love into our hearts by the Holy Spirit, whom he has given us* (Romans 5:3-5).

I love most of all the powerful illustration of the silversmith. The silversmith heats the silver again and again—each time skimming off the impurities until he can see his reflection in the shimmering crucible. In the same way, Jesus lovingly allows the heat in our lives to be turned up so that the impurities of our lives can be skimmed off and He can see His reflection in us. Perseverance leads to character.

Cleanse me from all unrighteousness. Wash me by the water of the Spirit and Word of God. Lord, give me the strength today to finish what You call me to. Give me grace to grow up in You—to mature in Your Spirit. Lord, it is my greatest desire to have all that You plan for me—to be all that You designed me to be—not lacking a thing. Amen

Wisdom

James 1:5

*If any of you lacks wisdom, he should ask God,
who gives generously to all without finding fault,
and it will be given to him.*

If any of you lacks wisdom? Those who deny
their need for wisdom have most certainly not
attained it. Who among us does not need to know
how to deal with this complex world we live in?
These can be very confusing times. As many
things as we are sure of, there are still more dilem-
mas—issues—situations that perplex us. We study,
but knowledge is not enough. We must have
wisdom. Even more important, we must have the
courage to act wisely—to make the right choice
once we have found the wise answer.

Where do you find the wisdom? James shares
with us a wonderful promise from the heart of
God. If you will seek, you will find that wisdom.
Jesus said: *Ask and it shall be given—seek and you
shall find—knock and the door shall be opened.*
But have you ever felt you were not even worthy
to ask? James suggests a remarkable thing—that
this wisdom is given by grace—"without finding
fault." Even in your most difficult and broken
times—when your mind is confused and clouded
with your own failure—God is faithful to this
promise and will give the wisdom needed. On the
worst day of your life—God's ears are not blocked
from hearing your cry. Our wise God is that good.

So how about today? Do you lack wisdom for today? Ask God. He gives generously to all. Without finding fault. And it will be given to you.

Lord, I do not know what this day holds—but You know the wisdom I shall need. Lord, give me the wisdom to know Your will and Your way. Give me also the courage to walk in that wisdom. Amen.

Believe

James 1:6

But when he asks, he must believe and not doubt,
because he who doubts is like a wave of the sea,
blown and tossed by the wind.

A recent poll by Luntz Research indicates that 10 percent of Americans believe that Elvis Presley is still alive, 30 percent believe in reincarnation, 39 percent believe in ghosts, 53 percent believe that aliens have visited earth in the past 100 years, 74 percent believe that the U.S. government is currently involved in cover-ups and conspiracies. It seems that we *believe* in a lot of things.

It is interesting that when the Bible talks about *believing*, the Greek word means *to cast your whole weight upon.* When we seek the wisdom and counsel of the Lord, we are not shopping for a convenient truth. We are not speculating about UFOs or Elvis. We are not even seeking in all manner of places some "wisdoms" that we will later choose from among the guidance of the worldly counsel. We are casting our whole weight upon the God of the universe and His wisdom. We *believe.*

Frankly, we do not have the option of hearing God's wisdom and then rejecting it. The very wisdom revealed will make us miserable if doubted and not acted upon. It is a miserable man or woman who knows the wisdom of God—and then has refused to walk in it.

Lord, I believe. Help my unbelief. I offer my faith to You—and sacrifice my doubt before Your throne. Teach me to walk by faith. Amen.

Double-M

James 1:7-8

That man should not think he will rec...
thing from the Lord; he is a double-minded...
unstable in all he does.

I love the scene in "Pirates of the Caribbean" at Disney World where the pirate is weighed down with treasure—stretched with one foot in the boat and one foot on the dock. He teeters back and forth. Each time he almost gets on shore, the weight of the treasure he clings to threatens to plunge him over the edge. It is obvious that at some point, he will have to make a choice. Boat or shore? Treasure or safety?

Our journey with God is much like that. We ask—but without really believing. We like to have God in our lives as a kind of safety net—but we cling to the world and its ways. James calls this "double-minded." It describes the schizophrenic way we sometimes try to live a life both of the Kingdom and of the world. We ask for wisdom and guidance—and then do as we please. "Double-minded" describes the energy we sometimes pour into hiding a secret sin, or defending our private rebellion while we try to keep up a good religious front. The truth is that we are kidding ourselves and we are above all—unstable. Kierkegaard said that purity of heart is to will one thing. James calls us to a purity of heart. James calls us to ask—seek—and find. General H.

man Schwarzkopf once said: "The truth of the matter is that you always know the right thing to do. The hard part is doing it." James would say: Just do it.

How about you? Have you been standing in between? Have you been teetering between the boat and the shore? Reaching for the Kingdom but clinging to the world? Have you known the right things but lingered in double-minded hesitation? Just do it.

Lord, help me to focus on You. Lead me to single-minded obedience that I may seek first the Kingdom of God and Your righteousness. Give me grace to know Your ways and courage to let go of this world. Amen.

High Position

James 1:9

The brother in humble circumstances ought to take pride in his high position.

James wrote at a time when the persecutions in Jerusalem were taking their toll. At one point the Christians in Jerusalem were near starvation and only the special offering collected by Paul pulled them through. In all this, James had discovered that there is great wealth—a "high position"—in humble circumstances.

This sounds strange to us in a culture that is obsessed with material things. We are bombarded by daily messages that tell us exactly the opposite—that our worth is measured by our clothing, cars, and the speed of our computers. In first century Galilee, the "things" were different—but the message was the same. In response, Jesus actually had the audacity to say that it is a blessing to be poor (Luke 6:30). How can that be? What does that mean? Certainly hunger and poverty are not "blessings." Perhaps the point was this: It is in our times of great need or difficult circumstance that we discover our need for God and utter dependence upon Him. These are great spiritual opportunities. This is when we grow. And it is in our times of leisure and abundance that we tend to drift from God.

The truth is—if you visit the tables of any Christian family in a third world country, you will hear the prayer: "Give us this day our daily bread..." said in a different sort of way than it is uttered around our tables of abundance. It is a lesson in how to pray those words. The prayer is pure. The prayer is real. James knew that Christian people going through hard times are, in fact, in the high position of the Spirit—a place of utter dependence upon God. We discover this in strange ways. Many times I have been astounded to hear Christian friends tell me of the huge blessing they have found in humble circumstances—the blessing they received when they lost a job but found their family—the blessing of a lost fortune and a rediscovered dependence upon God—the blessing of a trial that brought estranged people back together. God uses the hard times. No doubt about it. And there is wealth untold in the humble circumstances. In fact, the "good times" are often our greatest distraction.

So where are you today? Have you been missing the high position? These are times to draw near to God. It may be that the truly difficult times—the times of abundance—are just ahead.

Lord, I give thanks to You for the humble circumstances I have experienced in life. Help me to discover my spiritual poverty that I may draw near to You. Strengthen me for the times of abundance when it will be easy to drift from You. Give us this day our daily bread. Amen.

Low Position

James 1:10-11

But the one who is rich should take pride in his low position, because he will pass away like a wild flower. For the sun rises with scorching heat and withers the plant; its blossom falls and its beauty is destroyed. In the same way, the rich man will fade away even while he goes about his business.

The world says that material wealth is the answer. If we can just find wealth—we will have the high position—on top of the world. But there is increasing evidence that worldly wealth does not satisfy. In America, we live in perhaps the most affluent culture ever to occupy the planet. Americans have more disposable income today than at any other time. Yet, the percentage of monthly income used to pay consumer debts has risen from 16 percent in 1982 to over 29 percent in 1996. We don't seem to find satisfaction in the most affluence ever. The number of families filing for nonbusiness bankruptcies has tripled in that same time. The percentage of household income given to charities is at an all time low—and the largest percentage given to charities comes from households with incomes under $10,000 (Sources: First Chicago NDB; University of Wisconsin, Madison; American Bankruptcy Institute; and cdb Infotek; Gallup Organization for Independent Sector all cited in Chicago Tribune 10/10/96.)

James is clear that the place of affluence—

while certainly a place used by God—is the low position. Why? Perhaps it is because to have wealth in this world is to have been entrusted with the lesser of the treasures. Earthly treasure is important in eternity only in that stewardship is an important part of character. But even meeting church and personal needs in material ways—as important as they are—is on the lower rungs of God's economy—since all this is passing away. To be a steward of a spiritual gift, or the steward of spiritual matters, the steward of faith that trusts God while in difficult times, the steward of a soul, the steward of God's vision—these are the larger matters.

Lord, help me to be a good steward of both the worldly wealth and the Kingdom wealth that You have entrusted to me. Help me to focus today on what is eternal. Amen.

Crown

James 1:12

*Blessed is the man who perseveres under trial,
because when he has stood the test, he will receive
the crown of life that God has promised to those
who love him.*

Who can forget the images of the 1996 Summer Olympics? Incredible athletic efforts—records set—and the drama of awarding the medals. The very best and finest of efforts were honored in those ceremonies with pride and tears.

In the ancient world, the games were familiar as well. But for the Greek Olympian, the crown was not made of precious metal—it was a simple olive wreath that would begin to decay immediately. The ancients were wise. They realized that as soon as victory in this earthly realm was achieved—it was gone. The champion was winner for the day and that day only. As soon as the victory was won—there was someone a little faster or a little younger coming to overtake the victory.

James is quick to point out that this is not so with the victories of the Kingdom. The prize in this arena of competition is a crown of life. It is eternal. Even the gold, silver and bronze of the modern Olympic era are passing away. But we compete for a prize that is imperishable. What an image! The book of Hebrews describes it by telling us that we are surrounded by a great cloud of witnesses. The grandstand is full—as people of faith cheer us on toward the goal. If we could only hear their encouraging roar. But we will have to settle for the encouraging words of our Lord and for the encouragement of those, like James, who persevered in difficult times. Keep on! Reach out for that crown of life that God has promised to those who love Him!

Where are you today in the race? Lagging a bit? Grown a bit weary? Listen for the cheers from the stands. You are reaching out for a crown that lasts.

Lord, by Your grace, forgetting what lies behind, I press on toward the goal to win the prize for which You have called me heavenward in Christ Jesus. Amen

Tempting and Testing

James 1:13-14

When tempted, no one should say, "God is tempting me." For God cannot be tempted by evil, nor does he tempt anyone; but each one is tempted when, by his own evil desire, he is dragged away and enticed. Then, after desire has conceived, it gives birth to sin; and sin, when it is full-grown, gives birth to death.

It was the day before Christmas. I found myself puzzling over this verse. Who could talk about temptation today? *Nothing tempting on this day?* Store windows stuffed with goodies for everyone: Barbie dolls and basketballs, emerald bracelets and electronic games, exotic cheeses and chocolate angels. *Everything tempting on this day!* But James was talking about more than just the malls and food trays that make our holidays difficult. He was talking about the really tough places of temptation—real struggle with serious sin.

A mature Christian knows that such places of temptation are actually places where we grow a lot. A whole lot. There is little in the life of the Spirit that is as empowering as victory over the enticement of sin. No wonder some in the first century were saying—"God tempted me so I would grow!" But nothing could be further from the truth. Oh, the testing is allowed by God, to be sure. But the tempting itself is never from God.

James is bold in this introspection. No, we must not plead, "the devil made me do it." We must confess our own evil desires. We actually know the drill: After desire has conceived, it gives birth to sin; and sin, when it is full-grown, gives birth to death. Yet somehow in our human arrogance we think we can play with desire—but it drags us away. Sin and death—a separation from God—are the result. God would never tempt us toward that! He actually can't do that—He can only draw us to Himself. But on that road toward God—God can lead us—or allow us—into the place of testing.

The Scripture is clear about that. The Spirit of God led Jesus into the desert to be tempted (Lk. 4:1-2). *God knows that, at times, it is the only place where we will find ourselves.* Jesus taught that temptation was a place we should go only if there is no other way. He instructed us to pray: *Lead us NOT into the place of temptation—but deliver us from the evil one.* (Matthew 6:13). For Jesus—tempted in the desert—it was a time to rebuke the tempter with God's Word. For us, it is likely the same. *Submit yourselves, then, to God. Resist the devil, and he will flee from you* (James 4:7).

Paul seemed to have a grasp of the struggle and how to find victory when he wrote to the church at Corinth: *No temptation has seized you except what is common to man. And God is faithful; he will not let you be tempted beyond what you can bear. But when you are tempted, he will also provide a way out so that you can stand up under it* (1 Cor. 10:13). There is always a way out.

Tempted lately? Hang in there. The victory will make you strong.

Lord, lead me not into the place of temptation—but as I find myself there, let me stand up to the test and see Your way out—let me learn quickly what it is You want me to learn in every trial of life I encounter. Make me into whom You want me to be. Amen.

Gifts

James 1:16-17

*Don't be deceived, my dear brothers. Every good
and perfect gift is from above, coming down from
the Father of the heavenly lights, who does not
change like shifting shadows.*

We are a culture of gift givers. Christmas is
full of the obsession, but don't forget birthdays and
weddings and graduations!   Some gifts are from
Wal-Mart—others made by hand. Some gifts are
quickly returned while others will be cherished.
Some people will spend hours upon hours searching for the "perfect gift" in stores and catalogues.
But James has a warning.

Here is the warning: Do not be deceived. It
is so easy to be deceived and miss the perfect gifts
altogether.

I wonder: If James—the brother of Jesus—
came to visit, would he be a bit confused by one of
our typical Christmas celebrations—honoring the
birthday of Jesus? Would he be puzzled by our
frantic last minute rushing and searching? He
might find even more curious our common post-
Christmas let down, the feeling we often have after
Christmas—that we missed something.

You see—for James—the perfect gifts are so
obvious. They do not come from human hands.
They are never sullied by the markup of the
merchant. They are not trendy. The perfect gifts

do not change like shifting shadows. The perfect gifts come down from the Father of the heavenly lights. They are the gift of life. They are the gifts of faith, hope and love. The gift of salvation. The gift of comfort and strength from God's Holy Spirit.

Looking for the perfect gift? Look next to you. Stretch out your hand. Look inside your heart at the presence of Jesus—the Holy One of God. The good gifts—the perfect gifts come from God—all the rest is imitation joy—kind expressions, but never more than a vague reflection of the real thing.

Lord, let me see the things today that are really important. Thank You for the perfect gifts You have carefully prepared for me and my family. Give me the grace to open those gifts with joy and thanksgiving. Amen.

First Fruits

James 1:18

He chose to give us birth through the word of truth, that we might be a kind of firstfruits of all he created.

Do you remember that absolutely luscious taste of the first strawberry of spring? Was there anything more mouth-watering than the first watermelon of summer? The ancient Israelites reserved the firstfruits for dedication to the Lord— the first of the wheat harvest, the firstborn of the flock, the firstborn son. According to James, in Christ we are the first fruit of God's creation to be redeemed.

James tells us something even more profound—that God chose us. We are a chosen people. In our perspective of free will and stubborn self-reliance we often miss the degree to which our birth was the choice of God. Yes, we choose God, but not until long after He has chosen us. Yes, we pursue God in all the endeavors of life—all the way until He catches us. In other words—we are not an accident. We are uniquely created and uniquely reborn in Christ through the Word of Truth. It is the Word of God that brings us into contact with the Truth. God's Word does not return empty. So our redemption is never a source of pride or arrogance—or an opportunity to judge or malign. The larger purpose of God is a great work of redemption.

And just how does that happen? Jesus is the Word. Jesus is the Truth (John 14:6). Redemption comes in that personal encounter with Jesus. James called the recipients of this letter the "first fruits." The interesting thing about first fruits in the Hebrew culture was that they were always sacrificed at the Temple. These folks were going through tough times—but their sacrifice would not be in vain. The sacrifice of the firstfruits to the Lord is our act of faith that says—I trust that God is not finished and is going to do more. There is more blessing to come. We are the first fruits. Intended to be a light to the world. But only as we offer ourselves back to Him.

Like the Israelites of old, let us offer our firstfruits—our best—to the Lord. Offer your day—your very life—to Him.

Lord, make me new through Your Word of Truth. Allow me to recognize Your hand in life as well as Your purpose. Allow me to be offered for Your glory. Amen.

New Ways

James 1:19

My dear brothers, take note of this: Everyone should be quick to listen, slow to speak and slow to become angry, for man's anger does not bring about the righteous life that God desires.

James suggests a great way to start your day—*Resolve to listen more—talk less—don't be as angry.* What simple wisdom.

Listen. The Kingdom really needs more listeners. The ministry of listening is a gift even if it isn't listed in Paul's letters. It may be one of the greatest gifts we ever offer to others and to God. Stop and listen to the people around you—your family—your friends—your fellow church members. Really hear from their lives—the joys and frustrations. Don't jump in with words. It is a careful discipline to listen, and one that values people as Jesus does. So many times Jesus stopped and listened to the lives of those around Him.

Talk less. So many times we wish we could get the quick words back. Words often ring and echo and sting—sometimes for years. Sometimes Jesus' most powerful messages were said with silence.

Anger slowly. You know—there is a place for anger. Jesus got angry, to be sure. There is a righteous indignation when the people or things of

God have been wounded or offended. But the anger of man—the selfish prideful *"I'm going to get my way"* bullish anger? That anger never brings us to where God wants us. Be slow to anger. Ask the deep questions about your anger. *"What am I really angry about? Am I really directing anger at the right things? Is this an anger I can responsibly express?"*

How about it? Willing to try?

Lord, open my ears—and my heart to listen. Open my mouth only with Your words. Open my relationship to Your reconciling love. Stir in me— ever so slowly—only holy and righteous anger. Amen.

Get Rid of it

James 1:21

*Therefore, get rid of all moral filth and the evil
that is so prevalent and humbly accept the word
planted in you, which can save you.*

James has already spoken beautifully about
the blessings of God when we need wisdom and
strength—about the provision of the Lord when we
are going through very difficult times of trial—
about the goodness of God to give great gifts. But
now there is some basic business to settle. It is not
for those partly committed or casually interested in
the life of the Spirit.

Given the graciousness of God—our response
is to *separate ourselves from moral filth—and evil.*
This is not about legalism that attempts to earn a
self-righteousness—this is about living in holiness
that responds to the love of Jesus. Moral filth and
evil are incompatible with the Word planted in us.
The Word planted—or engrafted—in us cannot
grow and transform us properly as long as we
compromise with things that work against that
Word.

Is there moral filth in your life? James gives
us the only solution—*get rid of it.* It is not something to toy with. There can be no compromise.
Perhaps we don't have any of the really bad stuff
that James it talking about. But do you suppose
James is also talking about the movies we watch—
the television we view—even the web sites we

visit? James says—*get rid of it.* All of it. And what about the more subtle places where the enemy has gained a foothold? The jokes told with certain friends—the inside humor or the latest sitcom innuendo—our tendency to accept more and more. James says—*get rid of it.* Why? Because it will eat you alive.

James is clear about "...*the evil that is so prevalent...*" We often excuse our own evil because of the prevalence of worse evil. But God does not grade on a curve. If we slowly tolerate more and more in our own lives because of our culture, we are sinking—rather than pulling up the world around us. We become numb to selfishness—self-centeredness—materialism—and self indulgence in a world that is always a good deal worse that we are. James says—get rid of it.

Is there something you need to get rid of today? Something you have grown accustomed to? Something you have tolerated too long? The very best day to clean house is—today.

Lord, illumine my house by the light of Your Holy Spirit. Reveal that which is unacceptable to You even though it may be readily accepted by the world. Give me courage to get rid of it. In Jesus' name. Amen.

Listening and Doing

James 1:22-24

Do not merely listen to the word, and so deceive yourselves. Do what it says. Anyone who listens to the word but does not do what it says is like a man who looks at his face in a mirror and, after looking at himself, goes away and immediately forgets what he looks like.

We probably live in the most "Word rich" generation of Christians in history—and yet we are among the most spiritually impoverished. The Word of God has never been more available—more interpreted—more translated in history. We have the Bible in multiple versions—with CD ROM search features—set to music on digital recordings—and playing 24 hours a day with beautiful pictures on television. But none of that wealth of Word makes any difference if we only LISTEN and never DO the Word.

The problem is that we are quick to see what that mirror of the Word shows—only to dash away without applying the soap and water also there that can make our faces clean! We are correctly diagnosed by the Physician—but we are without prescription or cure—even though the medicine is readily available and offered freely. You see—nothing reveals who we are more than this Word.

Nothing confronts our facades and illusions more than an encounter with Him. Nothing reveals the deepest needs of our lives more than this Word—which then actually fills those needs.

At the most profound moment in history, the Word became flesh—in the person of Jesus Christ—but that Word also becomes flesh each day when we submit to that Word in our lives. We become the living Word—the Body of Christ. It starts with a day in the Word—and a day with the Word in you.

So how about it? Take a look in that mirror. What do you see? Some spots you had been missing with the wash cloth? How about that stuff stuck on your teeth? Isn't it about time to clean up?

Lord Jesus, I desire to walk in obedience to You and Your Word. Show me the places that have grown dirty with neglect and wash me with Your Word. Give me the courage to not walk away. In Jesus' name. Amen.

Law and Grace

James 1:25

But the man who looks intently into the perfect law that gives freedom, and continues to do this, not forgetting what he has heard, but doing it—he will be blessed in what he does.

We really struggle with this thing of Law and Grace. Paul makes it clear that we are not and cannot be saved by the Law. Only by Grace are we saved. It seems that the Law functions mostly to reveal how sinful we are—and how desperately we need God. But Law also functions in another paradox—to give us freedom.

Think about it. A society without any law is not a free society—it is enslaved to the barbarism of human depravity. Without law—no one is free. In much the same way, the Law of God offers an option of freedom—simply by telling us that there is another way to live. Oh, we cannot live that freedom apart from the power of Holy Spirit—but without the Law, we would not know there is any other choice at all. The perfect Law reveals the darkness—so that we can then choose the light.

The perfect Law reveals the sickness—so that we can then choose health. The perfect Law reveals the despair—so that we then know to choose joy. James says that if we—in the power of the Spirit—DO this perfect Law—there is freedom and blessing. The blessing—notice—is not FROM what we do—but IN what we do—"he will be blessed in what he does." We do not earn blessing by being good—rather—we are actually blessed in the life of holiness. That is the Law that frees. We are wise to learn that we cannot live under Law— but also that we cannot find life without it.

Thank You, O God, for Your perfect Law. Thank You for revealing darkness and then sending Light. Thank You for revealing sickness and then offering healing. Thank You for revealing despair so that I might choose Joy. Thank You for the freedom in Your perfect Law. In Jesus' name. Amen.

Tongue

James 1:26

If anyone considers himself religious and yet does not keep a tight rein on his tongue, he deceives himself and his religion is worthless.

I think it is a conspiracy. Every time we go to ride horses, I get the wild one. The cowboy comes out with the last horse. As it jerks its head up and down, he says: "Now this one is a bit 'spirited.'" I know what that means. It mean I am going to be horizontal. It means bushes and trees. It means the William Tell Overture. I have learned that the "spirited horse" hates the tight rein. It is not content to plod along the trail. It snorts and jerks its head with resentment.

James points to the reality that the tongue can be every bit as "spirited" as that wild horse. Have you heard the old saying? *What you DO speaks so loudly, I cannot hear what you are saying.* A sobering truth especially among religious people. James goes even further in confronting us religious folk. *What you SAY—contradicts all the religion you DO.* Good works are easy compared to tongue control. Moral living is a piece of cake by comparison. Rules are easy to follow—as long as we can talk about those who do not follow them.

There is a lot of talk these days about a "religious spirit." Such a spirit seems to strive to deceive believers into thinking they can justify themselves—and then judge others who do not obey the religious rules. A lot of that takes place when there is a "spirited" and "unreigned" tongue loose and running down the path. James has straight talk for this. He had heard it all over the years from his place of leadership in Jerusalem. He had seen the religious spirit of the Pharisees—and that of self-righteous Christians. The restraint or lack of restraint of the tongue could tell all. If there is no rein on the tongue? That religion is worthless.

How is your reign on your tongue? Do you ever reflect on the day and cringe a bit at what came out of your mouth? Sometimes we are not even the best judge. It is a risky but revealing thing to ask a really trusted friend— *"How is the reign on my tongue? Do I hurt people? Wound others? Snap at those I love?"*

Lord, Jesus, I surrender my tongue to You. I pray that all I do and believe may not be contradicted by what I say. Rein in my tongue, O Holy Spirit of God. In Jesus' name. Amen.

True Religion

James 1:27

Religion that God our Father accepts as pure and faultless is this: to look after orphans and widows in their distress and to keep oneself from being polluted by the world.

I visited one of our missionaries in Guatemala recently. He told me about how hard it can be to coordinate groups that come from the United States to work. One team, he recalled to me, arrived, and as he began to direct them to the construction site for a new school—the visitors were suddenly uncomfortable with the plan. They explained that they did not come all this way to build a school— they came to do street preaching and witnessing. They were there to win souls—anyone could lay block.

Now don't misunderstand. No one has more passion for souls than this particular missionary. No one. But he had learned early in his mission work this message we hear from James. There are some practical parts of Christian mission that must come first. People who cannot read—cannot grow personally in God's Word. Third world people who are illiterate are usually also hungry. There are desperate human needs that preaching on a street with a megaphone will not begin to touch. A religion that would notch its belt with souls won while ignoring human needs—the widows and orphans—is—well—not "pure and faultless" according to James. We will leave it at that.

The truth is that day-to-day life in the Spirit will set us face-to-face with day-to-day human needs and concerns. To whom will Jesus guide us first? The prominent possible convert? The exciting new ministry? The wealthy new family? Actually—Jesus will guide us first to those who have no one else. Widows and orphans were the most needy of James' community who were often abandoned to their circumstance. In essence—James says: *"I can always measure your church simply by watching the way you treat the widows and orphans."* It is a truth that James surely learned from his brother Jesus—who said: *"If you have done it unto the least of these, you have done it unto Me."*

Who are the widows and orphans today? Not just those who are alone because of the circumstance of death. Many are abandoned by other circumstances and the ravages of our culture. The single moms. The single dads. The kids who don't have a mom or a dad at home. The needs may be more spiritual than economic. Whatever the case—REAL expression of religion—a genuine faith relationship with God in Jesus Christ—will start here.

Lord, whom have I been missing? Is there someone You have put in my path that You desire for me to love—support—care for—or give to? Lord, give a faith relationship and faith walk that is pure and faultless. Amen.

Favoritism

James 2:1-4

My brothers, as believers in our glorious Lord Jesus Christ, don't show favoritism. Suppose a man comes into your meeting wearing a gold ring and fine clothes, and a poor man in shabby clothes also comes in. If you show special attention to the man wearing fine clothes and say, "Here's a good seat for you," but say to the poor man, "You stand there" or "Sit on the floor by my feet," have you not discriminated among yourselves and become judges with evil thoughts?

One of the wisest bits of advice I ever received from a great pastor and mentor was this: *"It is better not to know what anyone gives to the church."* I was young and green, but I took the advice. I discovered in those training years that I never wanted to drive any faster—return a phone call more quickly—or respond any differently to a person in need—based upon that individual's wealth or prestige.

Over the years I had many others advise just the opposite. *"The pastor needs to know who the big givers are"*—said one denominational executive. In one church, I was handed a list of five names upon arrival as a new pastor and told these were my "first visits." When I asked, *"Why? Are they sick?"* I was told that they were the top five givers in the church. James would have choked on such actions. *"Have you not discriminated among yourselves and become judges with evil thoughts?"*

The first advice from my pastor and mentor was the best. I learned over the years that we are too frail as humans not to respond differently when we know either "money" or "power" is at stake. The truth is that we are all susceptible—not just pastors. Little has changed from the old days of synagogue life. It is easy to pay a little better attention to the well dressed and apparently well placed—even if outward appearances are more a facade today than ever.

But the issue is deeper than that. We are not to be respecters of persons—pandering to the images and prestige of this world. Why? Because Jesus is not a respecter of persons. When people come to the body of Christ—there is no one with higher rank or distinction—no one valued more highly than another. The price of salvation for a person we might look down on is just as high for Jesus as for any other. He paid the bill for that which is eternal. Until we can actually afford to purchase a single drop of the Savior's blood—we have no business declaring one person more valuable than another. It is a price we can never meet.

Now, frankly, that will get you into trouble in some circles. In many places the expectation is high that those who give a lot or have wealth are treated with favoritism—the special seat—a special visit—the brass plaque—the special banquet. Not in the Kingdom. Just the opposite is true. In the Kingdom— *"When you do it unto the least of these—you have done it unto me..."* No favoritism. Period.

Lord, forgive me. Forgive me the times I have thought one person more valuable than another. Forgive me the judgments—sometimes in favor of wealth—at other times against wealth. Give me eyes to see through it all. Eyes to see people as You do—in need of Your grace. Amen.

Rich and Poor

James 2:5-7

Listen, my dear brothers: Has not God chosen those who are poor in the eyes of the world to be rich in faith and to inherit the kingdom he promised those who love him? But you have insulted the poor. Is it not the rich who are exploiting you? Are they not the ones who are dragging you into court? Are they not the ones who are slandering the noble name of him to whom you belong?

It was an unusually cold winter. The family that came by the church was just the last in a stream of people that year coming by wanting help. Some had been hucksters. Some had genuine needs. Each time I helped someone, I prayed that God would not allow my heart to be hardened to those in genuine need just because of the few who are cons.

This guy seemed particularly sincere when he told me his story about losing everything when the plant in his town closed up North. Two kids asleep in the back of an old station wagon amid what looked to be everything this family owned seemed to attest to the story. The wife seemed too embarrassed even to talk. They both seemed genuinely shamed by the whole thing. It was "something they had never done before"—asking for help. All they wanted was some gas and a little food. I believed them.

As I filled the tank at the 7-Eleven store, I was

struck by the innocence of this sleeping child—illuminated by neon light in her slumber. How easily she could be my own daughter if only circumstances were a little different. Then the man came out of the store carrying the food bought on my credit card. It wasn't much but I would turn in the receipt to the church treasurer. The man thanked me—and put out his hand. Most don't do that—they move quickly on their way once they have their gas and food. It took me back for just a moment—then I shook his hand and he was on his way.

I don't think he knew or noticed that split second when I hesitated to grasp his hand. But I knew. Later Jesus made it clear to me. It was actually His hand—the hand of Jesus that I hesitated to touch—albeit briefly.

Conviction. James speaks words that are convicting in those moments when we treat the poor with anything but respect. Sure—there are times we cannot help. The poor actually respond well to honesty. (The cons are often revealed at this point.) James points out that those who are poor—are poor only in the eyes of the world—and are chosen to be rich in faith and to inherit the kingdom. Perhaps this is because people who have nothing often live very close to God. Very dependent. Such people may teach us some things about prayer—and trust—and stewardship.

Yet our culture is in awe of the rich—who often know very little of God. Hmmmm. What a mixed up world it can be. Thank you, James, brother of Jesus—for reminding us.

Lord, forgive me for averting my eyes—for looking with judgment at those who are hurting—for mixing up the priorities of life and missing those who are really rich with the things of God. Give me Your eyes to see and Your heart to care so that I may care for others. Amen.

Grace

James 2:8-11

If you really keep the royal law found in Scripture,
"Love your neighbor as yourself," you are doing
right. But if you show favoritism, you sin and are
convicted by the law as lawbreakers. For whoever
keeps the whole law and yet stumbles at just one
point is guilty of breaking all of it. For he who
said, "Do not commit adultery," also said, "Do not
murder." If you do not commit adultery but do
commit murder, you have become a lawbreaker.

My guess is that James had seen it all. He had
grown up in the small town of Nazareth. He had
watched his brother rise from obscurity to meteoric
fame—and then end in a tragic death. Then James
personally met Jesus in resurrection reality. That
new beginning brought James to the big city—to
be a key leader in the first "mother church" in
Jerusalem. He saw the disputes between the first
Messianic believers—the "in town" believers and
the "out of town" believers—the Jerusalem Jews
and the Greek Jews. He had seen the little
struggles between the "charter followers" of
Jesus—and the new converts. One thing was for
sure—there could be no favorites. Favoritism just
did not fit this Kingdom of God message. Not
based on color—or ethnic origin—or wealth. Jesus
would have had no place for such a thing. Neither
would James. No favorites.

Favoritism really is one of the oldest family

games. Isaac had his favorite—Esau. Rebekah had hers—Jacob. Harmless family struggles, right? Wrong. Just ask some of the people in the Holy Land still sorting it out with rocks and tear gas—the descendants of Isaac and Ishmael, Esau and Jacob. Favoritism is a sin that ends in agony.

That is easy—but where do we play our favorites? Is it in family relationships? Or church relationships? Are some on our good list and some on our bad? Are there cliques and circles? An "in crowd" and an "out crowd"? Or do we just play favorites with ourselves? Is everything evaluated in terms of "me"? Good old-fashioned self-interest is the original form of favoritism.

James has such a simple instruction. It is exactly what Jesus said—an extension of our love for God: Love your neighbor as yourself. Favoritism is not found in treating others well—or in treating yourself well—but in NOT treating everyone with value—failing to love as we all would desire to be loved. Favoritism is overcome when we treat everyone with the favor of God. That is not favoritism—that is grace.

Lord, who have I been missing or overlooking in my quest to share Your love? Help me to see the blind spots and share Your love today in places I have been missing. Teach me to be a person of grace—sharing God's favor. Amen.

Mercy

James 2:12-13

*Speak and act as those who are going to be judged
by the law that gives freedom, because judgment
without mercy will be shown to anyone who has
not been merciful. Mercy triumphs over judgment!*

Ann, my wife and ministry partner, has a
wonderful saying: *Pray as though it all depends on
God—and work as though it all depends on you.*
She actually lives that out at pretty high velocity.
James might suggest to us something similar—*trust*
as though it all depends on *grace*—but *live* as
though your works will be *judged by the law*—
especially when it comes to mercy.

Sometimes we get a little lax in our dependence on grace—we take it for granted.
Bonhoeffer called it "cheap grace." Grace that
forgets how holy and merciful God is—and how
much mercy is required of those who have received mercy is "cheap grace." Every time I feel
that spirit of judgment coming on—that part of me
that rears up and says—"I am holy—and that
person is bad"—I must without fail—remember
that without Jesus I am as lost as any and every
sinner in this universe. But for the mercy of a
loving God—I am eternally lost—alone—and
separated from Him. He judged me guilty. But
then He sought me out. He never gave up. And if
I were the only one—He still would have given
everything for me. See? James is right. Mercy

triumphs over judgment! The question is—Can that same mercy triumph over judgment in my life?

Mercy triumphs in my life when I receive that mercy. Mercy also triumphs in my life when I extend His mercy. And that is a sacred synergy. Blessed are the merciful—for they shall receive mercy. How about your circle of life? Is there some mercy to receive? Is there some mercy to extend?

Lord, put me in touch with Your mercy today—as never before that I may extend that mercy in ways that triumph over judgment. Amen.

Faith in Action

James 2:14-17

*What good is it, my brothers, if a man claims to
have faith but has no deeds? Can such faith save
him? Suppose a brother or sister is without clothes
and daily food. If one of you says to him, "Go, I
wish you well; keep warm and well fed," but does
nothing about his physical needs, what good is it?
In the same way, faith by itself, if it is not accompanied by action, is dead.*

We can almost imagine James trying to hold
together things in Jerusalem. There—with Peter
and other Apostles—managing a movement now
ten or fifteen years old. They had dealt with the
first big issue of accepting Gentiles (Acts 15). But
now economic times were rough. If not for the
offerings sent by Paul, a converted persecutor, they
never would have made it through the hard Jerusalem winters. Oh, there were lots of people who
came through town on the Jesus bandwagon.
They came to see the Apostles—so they could say
they had the "Apostolic blessing"—only to move
on with their new found "faith" to preach and
make their fortunes—and leave a lot of needs
behind.

Antioch was fast becoming the big church
everyone was talking about. The new mega
movement. But who was left in Jerusalem to care
for the aging widows of Jerusalem? They had
prayed for Messiah all their lives and finally had

found Him. But now they were aging—those first believers. And there were orphans—left to the streets by violence and disease. Oh, for the glory days of Pentecost when miracles were plentiful. Or is this where real faith is lived out? In the hard times. The faith that works is the faith that *works*.

True—this salvation of Jesus is by grace—as Paul was preaching. Salvation is *not* by the works of the law that so long ruled religious culture. BUT—and it is a very important "BUT"—*BUT what good is it, my brothers and sisters, if someone claims to have faith but has no deeds?* Is that faith real? Can such faith—that has brought no real change—no real compassion—be real—or save anyone? Suppose a brother or sister is without clothes and daily food. If one of you says to him, "Go, I wish you well; keep warm and well fed," but does nothing about his physical needs, what good is it? "I'll keep you in prayer" just doesn't cut it when it is thirty degrees outside and you are hungry. It is worse than no religion at all. Better not to claim the name of Christ than to claim that name and then live in a way that represents it as powerless and empty. Faith by itself, if it is not accompanied by action, is dead faith.

How are your vital stats in the faith department? The blood pressure, temperature and blood gases of our spiritual life are measured by the way faith is lived out. Is your faith alive today? Dead? On a respirator? There is a Physician who can help.

Lord, Jesus. I want faith that is alive. I want faith that is a relationship—that lives and breathes—and listens—and responds. I want to have faith marked by Your heart—Your compassion. Break me free, Lord. Keep my lips free from words of polite religious comfort. Lord, whisper in my ear today—and I will obey. Let me speak the Good News—but also let me live the Good News. Amen.

Faith in Deed

James 2:18

But someone will say, "You have faith; I have deeds." Show me your faith without deeds, and I will show you my faith by what I do.

For the first year that our church was in existence we worshipped in a simple rented facility used during the week by a private school. God was teaching us a great deal about humility and servanthood. Because of the difficulty of schedules, we had to clean much of our rented building as we came in for weekend services and then clean it all again as we left. There were lots of struggles in trying to share space with the classroom teachers who used the rooms during the week. We tried very hard to clean and put things back in order in order to avoid conflicts. Sometimes it seemed that we were doing much more than our fair share of custodial work and clean up. But the Lord spoke to my heart a truth. *We are the only Jesus many of these people will ever encounter.*

I am sure that we did not do a perfect job in those relationships—but it really convicted me that we were to do our work as unto the Lord. We were to serve these people—and clean their classrooms—as a testimony. It would be perhaps the only way we would be able to share our faith.

When we finally had an opportunity to move to a new location—we gave special floral gifts to each teacher and gift certificates to the school administrators as a farewell. God made it clear that while we would not be able to talk easily about our faith with those who shared space with us—when we left they would have either a positive or a negative image of us and of Christ whom we represent. I am sure that we fell short in many ways—but we sought to be positive ambassadors for Christ. I think that is something of what James was talking about when he said: *Show me your faith without deeds, and I will show you my faith by what I do.* There are times when our faith is not something we talk about—or beliefs we profess—faith is what some people will see lived out. Actions really do speak louder than words.

How is the Jesus you are showing to the world around you today? Is that Jesus a clear reflection of the Lord and Creator of the universe who has sought you and saved you? Or is that image a bit clouded because you have gotten in the way?

Lord, help me to live out my faith today in ways that will honor and glorify You. Write upon the activities of my life the Creed and Doctrine of New Life in You. Amen.

Shema

James 2:19

You believe that there is one God. Good! Even the demons believe that—and shudder.

James had grown up since childhood hearing and speaking the "Shema" the most sacred prayer of Israel: *Hear, O Israel: The Lord our God, the Lord is one. Love the Lord your God with all your heart and with all your soul and with all your strength* (Deut. 6:4-5). This is the most precious verse in all of Judaism and the foundation of Hebrew faith. A copy of this verse is placed in the a small leather box worn by orthodox men during prayer—and the same is put into the small container on the doorframe of each Jewish home. It is the centerpiece of Jewish faith.

In ancient times this was the key doctrinal distinctive—belief in the One True God. But now James seems to be saying that this is not enough. Or is he? The first word of the treasured text is the word *shema*—or *hear*. The word is a rich one and means to *hear intelligently—and with obedience—to give complete attention with perception and diligence and then to proclaim—even give witness.* This is more than just a call for simple attention—it is a call to hear and respond with all of your being.

James may have been concerned that the depth of that Hebrew meaning had been lost. It is so easy to slip into the habit of "beliefism"—reciting creeds or affirming doctrine—but missing something that is critical. So he reminds us of the frightening reality that even demons are capable of doing that! It sounds strange but demons were among the first to recognize Jesus as the Son of God! (Luke 4:33-34) Intellectual assent to proper doctrine is important but it is only part of the journey. What is missing? Relationship. Genuine response. Shema.

More significant than any doctrine is the reality that God desires a living love relationship with us through the person and work of Jesus Christ. All the rules in the world will not create that relationship even if properly obeyed. All the doctrine and proper prayer forms will not achieve it. In many ways, it is like any other relationship—it begins with time together—joys shared—griefs comforted and honest communication. This relationship is a gift offered freely and renewable each and every day—but it must be attended to. The demons know the doctrine and they shudder—because they do not have the love relationship or trust that is the joy of living.

How is your shema? How is your hearing relationship with God? How is your obedient response? Your diligence to proclaim?

Lord, I want to know You today. I want to be aware of Your presence—creating and re-recreating me. I want to walk in a relationship where You guide and empower me to become whom You designed me to be. I hear—shema. You are One. Teach me to love You with all my heart and with all my soul and with all my strength. Amen.

Action in Faith

James 2:20-24

*You foolish man, do you want evidence that faith
without deeds is useless? Was not our ancestor
Abraham considered righteous for what he did
when he offered his son Isaac on the altar? You
see that his faith and his actions were working
together, and his faith was made complete by what
he did. And the scripture was fulfilled that says,
"Abraham believed God, and it was credited to
him as righteousness," and he was called God's
friend. You see that a person is justified by what
he does and not by faith alone.*

Faith is an amazing thing. It really does exist
free and clear of any action—but James observes
that we don't really know that—until the action is
there. For Abram, saying "*I surrender all*" did not
really take form until he truly did surrender all.
That is the story of faith. Peter totters at the edge
of the boat—Jesus is calling him out onto the
water. One foot is in the boat—the other hovers
over the foam. There is that split second when
weight is shifted from the boat side foot to the
water side foot and the one behind no longer
carries the weight. It is then—and only then—that
Peter knew for sure that God was indeed the
Master of the waves. You see that his faith and his
actions were working together, and his faith was
made complete by what he did.

Have you ever been there? Henry Blackaby
calls it a *crisis of belief* that requires faith and

75

action. It is that moment when God has spoken and we stop talking about faith and start walking with faith. It happened to me one day as I drove down the road in serious confusion about where God wanted me in ministry. *"If You just provide a way—I will go"*—I prayed. But God responded in clarity to my heart— *"That is not faith."* I suddenly realized that while I had taught and preached faith—actually trusting God was another matter altogether. Remember that Greek word for "believe" or "faith"? It means "*to cast your whole weight.*" Faith is more than believing God CAN hold you. It is casting your whole weight upon Him. It is *this* faith that justifies—faith that evidences trust in the fruit of actions.

This is the faith that caused Levi to walk away from a good-paying job at a well-located tax stand. This is the faith that motivated several fishermen to leave their nets. This is the faith that compelled the Apostle Paul to make the best-known career change in ecclesiastical history. It is the faith that empowered Mary and Martha to have the tomb of their brother Lazarus opened after four days of decay. It is the faith that caused a sick woman to reach out of the crowd at all cost to touch the hem of His garment. It is faith that makes a difference.

How is your faith quotient? Is your faith more on the passive side? We usually raise that quotient one step at a time. What is God calling you to trust Him in today?

Lord, I desire to cast my whole weight upon You. Show me where You want me to go and how You want me to trust You today. Show me the one step You desire for me to take—be it ever so simple. Amen.

No Labels

James 2:25-26

In the same way, was not even Rahab the prostitute considered righteous for what she did when she gave lodging to the spies and sent them off in a different direction? As the body without the spirit is dead, so faith without deeds is dead.

Do you remember the story of Rahab? God had given the land of Canaan to the Hebrews. They finally were ready to take the land but Jericho stood in the way. Joshua sent two spies in to check things out. They would have been caught and tortured except for a pagan woman—a prostitute—named Rahab. She hid the spies based on her faith! She professed before them *"...the Lord your God is God in heaven above and on the earth below"* (Joshua 2:11).

But this was more than simple fear or even a verbal affirmation. Rahab hid the spies and misdirected the King so they could get away. Because of this she was spared in the conquest of Jericho. Later genealogies in the book of Judges show that she actually was grafted in as a part of the nation of Israel.

Just what does such faith do for you? James uses the word *righteous.* The Greek word means *"to be rendered innocent."* It is interesting that in every place that Rahab is mentioned in the Bible, including the book of James, Rahab carries the label: "Prostitute." In every place except one.

Rahab is listed in the lineage of Jesus in Matthew's Gospel—but with one difference. In that list—in the lineage of Jesus—*in Jesus*—grafted into that line—*there is no label.* That is what faith does—it puts us into Jesus where there are no labels.

We are grafted into the same lineage but as progeny rather than ancestry. Faith that trusts and obeys—puts us into the line of Jesus and removes the labels of life that attach themselves to us. Do you have a label? Something someone put on you—or that stuck from a long time ago? Labels are terrible and cruel things. *Poor, dumb, no-count, smart, failure, nerd, divorced, single, no good, old, young, unwed, bad, loose, cheap, unemployed?* On and on they go, these modern labels. The faith of Rahab—that trusts and obeys—that recognizes God and responds—that faith is what grafts us into Jesus where there is no label. Paul put it this way: *If anyone is in Christ, he is a new creation; the old has gone, the new has come* (2 Cor. 5:17). Celebrate that today.

Lord, Jesus, today I want to be in You—grafted in—part of Your ongoing lineage. I understand that no one in the lineage has any labels. There are no tax collectors or sinners. Lord, I want to walk in You today. Teach me to trust and obey. Make me a new creation. May the old pass away and the new come! Amen.

High Calling

James 3:1

Not many of you should presume to be teachers, my brothers, because you know that we who teach will be judged more strictly.

I have often struggled with this text because it makes it so hard to recruit Sunday School teachers! But then I wonder—after all—*do we not all teach?* With every gesture, word and action before observant children? In the way we respond in the work place? As we care for and attend to relationships that are important or difficult? We teach who Jesus is in our lives.

But James speaks of the official calling. In Judaism there were no preachers. They were teachers. Rabbis. Those who had been schooled carefully by question and answer—now would teach in the same way. Jesus was the Master Rabbi—bringing spiritual truth to life through parable and illustration. Honing the Word to its razor sharp point of truth so that it would penetrate the soul.

But James knew that teachers could get lax. There was so much respect for the Rabbi, yet Jeremiah also warned of the "false teachers" with their false prophecies and dreams. Jesus warned of the same. Remember, it was the teachers of the law—the legal experts—that had such a hard heart for the truth of God and sought to trap Jesus.

So James warns us. Don't presume to be a teacher without knowing you will be judged more strictly. It is a high calling. It is one thing to blunder in understanding some truth or another for yourself. It is quite another to lead others astray because of carelessness or laziness. Want to teach? Study. Pray. Study more. Pray harder. And if you have a really important class—no, not the one full of adults—the one with children—be extra careful and pray one more time that you have got it right.

Whom will you be teaching today?

Lord, teach through me today. In all that I do—be the Rabbi that is needed. And Lord, should You call me to a position of teaching—give me grace to study and pray hard. I will take it seriously. Amen.

The Tongue

James 3:2-5

We all stumble in many ways. If anyone is never at fault in what he says, he is a perfect man, able to keep his whole body in check. When we put bits into the mouths of horses to make them obey us, we can turn the whole animal. Or take ships as an example. Although they are so large and are driven by strong winds, they are steered by a very small rudder wherever the pilot wants to go. Likewise the tongue is a small part of the body, but it makes great boasts.

James has made a powerful point thus far. Christian faith is more than just talk—more than just belief—it is action. But now he turns things around. *Words are important, too!* You may act in a Christian manner—but the way you talk is most revealing. We can harness the appetites of the body—reign in evil desire—restrict all manner of sinful possibilities—but the real difficulty is controlling the tongue.

James is not even so concerned with the traditional misuse of the Lord's name. The concern is in those things we say that are so very powerful for good or evil. And controlling this part of the human animal is the height of mastery. It is true. What we say shapes so much of what goes on around us. We have choices—we really can choose either to speak negative possibilities into existence or speak an air of confidence and hope into the room. We really do pronounce blessings or curses upon those near to us. With every word of encouragement and hopeful expectation we participate with God in bringing out the very best of our family members, coworkers and church members. The right word at the right time makes all the difference in the world. Like the rudder of a ship, the gift of words—communication—is a steering force and a responsibility entrusted.

How about it? Will today be a day of great accomplishment—possibilities—hope—growing trust? You can choose to steer it that way.

Lord, I commit my mouth to You this day. All that I say—I pray—would be honoring to You. Speak through me words of hope—encourage-ment—expectation—confidence—into the lives of those around me. In Jesus' name. Amen.

Gossip

James 3:5-6

Consider what a great forest is set on fire by a small spark. The tongue also is a fire, a world of evil among the parts of the body. It corrupts the whole person, sets the whole course of his life on fire, and is itself set on fire by hell.

There is a rabbinical story told that a man came to a rabbi repentant for having told lies and malicious gossip about another person. The man had found forgiveness with the friend but wanted to make things right with God. The rabbi instructed the man to take a feather pillow to the town square—tear it open and scatter the feathers to the wind. The man did what he was told and then came back. The rabbi then instructed that in order to find forgiveness—he must retrieve every feather from across the town. (Wayne Dosick, *The Business Bible*, pp. 43-44.) It is a powerful story. Not because it teaches us about forgiveness and grace in Jesus Christ— but it illustrates the power of words to damage and the impossibility of retrieving them.

James makes the point with a different image. A spark sets a forest on fire. It is a scene we are familiar with during the dry season. No one even knows where the spark began but the winds fan a raging firestorm and thousands of square miles are scorched. Can James put it *any* stronger? It is not just malicious gossip—it is the negative word—the thoughtless outburst—the dumping of matters onto a Christian friend who simply does not need the burden.

How do we gain control of our tongue? Sometimes a "fast" on speaking is good. A season of quietness. Resolving simply not to speak for a while. Carefully realizing the power of *not speaking.*

Another way is not to give ear to it. When the gossip begins—respond differently. How do you suppose these comments would impact the world of gossip?

"Wait... Is this something that I can share with that person....?"

"Perhaps we should stop before you share another detail and just PRAY for that person..."

"This is a secret? Then I want YOU to keep it a secret! That way I will know you can keep my confidence in the future..."

"You know the other day—I realized later I sinned by gossiping to you and I would like to ask your forgiveness..."

"When we talked last time—I realized you were left with a terrible impression of our brother/sister in Christ—I would like to correct that."

"I want to confess to you that I have sinned by gossiping about you—will you forgive me?"

Why is there so much gossip even in Christian circles? For the same reason there is sleaze on television: Because there is a market for it! An appetite for tasty morsels. If Christians will shut down the market for gossip it will go away.

Lord, forgive me for the fires I may have started unintentionally. I pray for the scorched land to be healed. I cannot retrieve all the feathers, Father, but guide me to correct the most important. I commit myself to make those corrections. Fill me with Your Holy Spirit so that there is no hunger in me to say or hear that which is not of You. Whatever is true, whatever is noble, whatever is right, whatever is pure, whatever is lovely, whatever is admirable—if anything is excellent or praiseworthy—I commit myself to think about such things. Amen.

Fresh Waters

James 3:7-11

*All kinds of animals, birds, reptiles and creatures
of the sea are being tamed and have been tamed
by man, but no man can tame the tongue. It is a
restless evil, full of deadly poison. With the tongue
we praise our Lord and Father, and with it we
curse men, who have been made in God's likeness.
Out of the same mouth come praise and cursing.
My brothers, this should not be. Can both fresh
water and salt water flow from the same spring?
My brothers, can a fig tree bear olives, or a grapevine bear figs? Neither can a salt spring produce
fresh water.*

Playing back the tapes of memory can be a
frightening thing if we ever are quiet long enough
to do so. Often we realize that the very things we
never wanted to say—have just come from our
mouths. And the words of faith we thought we
could always proclaim anywhere got stuck in our
throats. This matter of the tongue is not easy.

But don't misunderstand—James is saying
more than just—"try harder." Taming the tongue is
not just a matter of stronger will power and more
resolve. *No one can tame the tongue.* Say that
again? No one—man or woman—can tame the
tongue. We are now bordering on hopeless! And
what a description—the tongue is restless? Evil?
Poison? And as religious people we are shocked to
hear both praise and curses coming from our own
mouths. What are we to do?

Paul described the same sort of struggle in a more general way with sin. To paraphrase Paul in Romans 7:15— *"I do not understand what I say. For what I want to say I do not say, but what I hate to hear I find rolling from my mouth."* So just what IS the answer? James gives the answer in a sort of classic rabbinical teaching style—the answer is in a question: *Can both fresh water and salt water flow from the same spring?* Of course not. The answer is that until the spring is fresh—you cannot expect anything but brackish water. Again—in case we did not get it—*My brothers, can a fig tree bear olives, or a grapevine bear figs?* Of course not. Until the actual *root* of the tree is changed—the fruit can never be anything different than its root.

What is the answer? A radical transformation. Not just fruit adjustment—not just a pail of fresh water. A *root change.* A *new spring.* The fruit of curses—or gossip—or rage—or coarse talk—or ethnic epithets—all these are fruit of something inside that is not surrendered to Jesus. Perhaps even a sign that spiritual renewal still needs to take place. The answer begins when we are born from above—but it does not stop there and results are not instantaneous.

I had a friend in high school who accepted Christ. He had been a vile-mouthed rebel. His first prayers to the Lord shocked me because even his prayers were peppered with profanity. But almost immediately the transformation began—without reprimand—or correction—*God cleaned up his mouth.* As the Spirit of the Holy God had His way in this life—my friend was sanctified—slowly made more like Jesus. The Spirit became clean and the mouth followed. God still does that. We can do nothing besides surrender to Him. God must do in us what He wills—cleansing—whether it is profanity or just mean spirited "Christian gossip." He is in the business of making all things new.

Create in me a pure heart, O God, and renew a right spirit within me. Cleanse me to-day—that pure water may run from the spring of my life. Place sweet fruit upon my lips that my words may bless and encourage and build. In Jesus' name. Amen.

Wisdom

James 3:13-18

Who is wise and understanding among you? Let him show it by his good life, by deeds done in the humility that comes from wisdom. But if you harbor bitter envy and selfish ambition in your hearts, do not boast about it or deny the truth. Such "wisdom" does not come down from heaven but is earthly, unspiritual, of the devil. For where you have envy and selfish ambition, there you find disorder and every evil practice. But the wisdom that comes from heaven is first of all pure; then peace-loving, considerate, submissive, full of mercy and good fruit, impartial and sincere. Peacemakers who sow in peace raise a harvest of righteousness.

We are a culture that is hungry for wise leadership and understanding. We crave someone with knowledge but thirst even more for someone with wisdom and understanding. But it is not that easy, is it? Half the list of best seller books claim to have both. The television is full of "spiritual leaders" and 900 number revelations. And the church scene is often not much better. What are we to do? With all this confusion, how will we know if we are listening to *true wisdom?* James tells us.

Leadership that has true wisdom is marked not just by words but *deeds done in humility*. No "photo ops" or "sound bites" here. No flashy mission segment in today's broadcast. You will have to watch carefully to catch true wisdom at work in humility. Quietly. No undue attention. Can you obey God in a completely anonymous and unselfish act? That is a mark of true wisdom.

Leadership that has true wisdom is NOT marked by bitter envy and selfish ambition. That is a red flag—the leader who spends a lot of time putting down others (a sure sign of envy!)—the leaders who define themselves by criticizing others—and who seem more concerned with their climb to prominence. Nope. These are sure signs something is wrong—earthly—unspiritual—and "of the devil," to be honest. There will be confusion—disorder.

True wisdom is *pure*—having no ulterior motives. That is something we may sense right away or even see as time goes on. True wisdom is *peace loving*. Like Jesus in the Garden of Gethsemene commanding swords be put away. True wisdom is *considerate*. Paul said love is not rude—neither is the wise leader. Rude attacks are never necessary—even when the "wise" attacker is correct. We never saw that in Jesus. True wisdom is *submissive?* The greatest leader is obviously a follower. *Followship is a prerequisite to leadership.* If a leader is not surrendered to God—he or she is not a Godly leader. Period. A wise leader is also not afraid to give in—to submit—to a better idea. Pride will not get in the way. True wisdom is *full of mercy.* Mercy is that quality of God that gives another chance and moves on—and even overlooks the "right to be right." True wisdom is *impartial.* No favorites here. Mercy for all. True wisdom is *sincere*. It is not something you can fake until you get the hang of it. It comes without masks.

Well—how do you measure up? Only by the grace of Jesus can all that take place? Exactly. Is it a little more clear whom you should follow? Good. Have a great day in Jesus.

Lord, give me Your wisdom and understanding. Lead me to quiet and humble acts that honor You alone. Make me pure, peace-loving, considerate, submissive, full of mercy and good fruit, impartial and sincere. I pray for a harvest of righteousness. Amen.

Fights

James 4:1-3

*What causes fights and quarrels among you? Don't
they come from your desires that battle within
you? You want something but don't get it. You kill
and covet, but you cannot have what you want.
You quarrel and fight. You do not have, because
you do not ask God. When you ask, you do not
receive, because you ask with wrong motives, that
you may spend what you get on your pleasures.*

James is talking to a mature Christian audience. But even among mature Christian people
there can still be disagreements—even fights and
quarrels. It can be even worse when we are at
odds with the world. There were some big issues
to be dealt with in the early church. Jewish Christians were in conflict with gentile Christians over
how much of the law to observe. Leaders like
Peter and Paul had sharp disagreements. Paul also
parted ways with his close friend and sponsor
Barnabas and his young follower John Mark. God
seemed to use those times of disagreement in a
positive way—but they had to be painful.

Perhaps there will always be some kind of
disagreement among Christian people of conscience. But James cautions us to be very careful
about such things. There is a fighting—a war-
ring—that comes from *selfish motivations and
wrong desires*. James cautions the Christian community to look carefully within—to discern the real

source of conflict. It there something within that is driving us? Something not of God? Is there some unmet need—or unknown motivation? Is there some bit of envy or covetousness hidden away? Or is it a matter of pride? Stubbornness? We can become set on having our way—and when we don't get what we want, the quarreling starts.

Surely there were no real murders among the Christian community—but remember that Jesus once said that if we call others degrading names—"You empty headed fool!"—it is like murder because we assassinate the character and name of that person in our hearts.

The answer is so simple. *You do not have the solutions to these conflicts because you do not ask God.* Do you really want peace? Have you asked God? Do you really want an answer—a real solution—or are you just set on getting your own way? Have you asked God? Even when we have gone to God—our motives have been impure and self centered—that is not the way to get the will of God in our lives. Motive matters.

How about a different day today? One where you look inside—and before you quarrel—or fight—you ask: What is really going on here? Why do I care about this? Is this really a fight that honors God? Or is the relationship with this person—in the end—more important than winning or getting my way? Something to think about.

Lord, You said that if I would delight myself in You—You would give me the desires of my heart. Lord, give me desires that honor You. Reshape the things that drive me. Remold my motivations. Show me the things you really want me to strive for this week. Amen.

Friendship with the World

James 4:4-6

You adulterous people, don't you know that
friendship with the world is hatred toward God?
Anyone who chooses to be a friend of the world
becomes an enemy of God. Or do you think
Scripture says without reason that the spirit he
caused to live in us envies intensely? But he gives
us more grace. That is why Scripture says: "God
opposes the proud but gives grace to the humble."

When we first read this verse, we might well
be stunned. Adulterous people? It is stinging.
Actually James is using an allusion that was familiar
in the Hebrew Scriptures. Stunning and strong—it
painfully describes those times when Israel fell
away. God was clear that this was nothing less than
spiritual adultery. After all, the Hebrew Scripture
describes Israel as the wife of God. *"They broke*
my covenant, though I was a husband to them,"
declares the Lord (Jeremiah 31:32). And don't
forget that the New Testament Scripture describes
the people of God as the bride of Christ—
(Ephesians 5:22-23). God views unfaithfulness as
adultery (Hosea 2:2-5; Hosea 3:1-5). *"Do not*

rejoice, O Israel; do not be jubilant like the other nations. For you have been unfaithful to your God; you love the wages of a prostitute at every threshing floor" (Hosea 9:1). It is a strong rebuke but one that makes very clear the pain that we cause God in our unfaithfulness.

God puts it into human terms that we can understand. But James goes further—even friendship with the world is "hatred" toward God? The word James uses is the same as "enemy"—or "satan"! Friendship with the world makes us "a satan" toward God? A harsh statement—but this is same way that Jesus referred to Peter when he suggested Jesus should not continue the path toward the cross (Matthew 16:23): *"Get behind me, Satan! You are a stumbling block to me; you do not have in mind the things of God, but the things of men."*

But how are we to reach a culture that is lost? Are we to withdraw to horse and buggy communities? Actually James is condemning those moments when we make an alliance of trust with the "kosmos" or the power structures of the world. James is making clear the incompatibility of worldly principalities and power with the Kingdom of God. The question is this: *Where do you really put your TRUST?* Trust is your friendship bond. You cannot be bonded in friendship—*trust*—both to God and to the "kosmos"—the world order.

Question of the day—How can I REACH my culture—without buying into its values or compromising to its power structures? Can I REACH my culture—without being seduced into spiritual adultery with it? God jealously longs for the spirit that He made to live in us. For that reason—He opposes the proud—those who trust worldly power—but He gives grace to the humble—those who trust in Him.

Lord, I love YOU and only You—with all my heart, soul, mind, and strength. I want to love my neighbor as myself. Forgive me any way that I may have given into the seductions of the power structures of this world. Show me how to live this day wholly for You. Give me Your grace. Amen.

Submit

James 4:7-10

Submit yourselves, then, to God. Resist the devil, and he will flee from you. Come near to God and he will come near to you. Wash your hands, you sinners, and purify your hearts, you double-minded. Grieve, mourn and wail. Change your laughter to mourning and your joy to gloom. Humble yourselves before the Lord, and he will lift you up.

The last word from James was rather harsh: "You adulterous people, don't you know that friendship with the world is hatred toward God? Anyone who chooses to be a friend of the world becomes an enemy of God" (James 4:1-2). So how do we RESPOND to such a strong word? James has an answer. SUBMIT TO GOD—RESIST THE DEVIL.

What could be more simple than that? But it seems that everything within us—our broken human nature—wants instead to do just the opposite. We get it turned around and RESIST GOD and SUBMIT TO THE DEVIL. Oh, we may not actually surrender the war to the devil but we surrender a lot of battles without a fight! Even as we claim Christ as Savior, it seems that the easy path—the path of least resistance—is this one. And what a miserable life that is! With Christ living inside us—we resist God—and then submit to the tempter and find ourselves at war within. So what is the answer? James cannot outline it more clearly.

Submitting to God works this way. First, resist the devil and HE WILL FLEE—he MUST—he WILL! It is a promise. Draw near to God— and He WILL draw near to you. (It does not say God might draw near—He WILL draw near.) When God is near— we are aware of our need to be cleansed (Isaiah 6:5). Next we ask God to purify our hands (the things we DO) and our hearts (our thoughts and motives). Both are vital. Of course there is a grief attached to this. True repentance grieves how we have hurt our relationship with God—how we have hurt ourselves and others. Finally, we humble ourselves before the Lord—and here is the great part—He WILL lift us up. That is real joy— when we are LIFTED by the Lord. But there is only one road that gets us there. We cannot detour or take a quick course. True repentance that draws near to God—seeks to be clean in actions and motives—grieves—humbles—and is set free.

Lord—as an act of my will—I am drawing near to You right now. Reveal to me the areas of life that I have too easily surrendered to the enemy—cleanse me, O God. Cleanse my actions and my thoughts. I am humbled before You. Lift me up, O God. Amen.

Slander

James 4:11-12

*Brothers, do not slander one another. Anyone who
speaks against his brother or judges him speaks
against the law and judges it. When you judge the
law, you are not keeping it, but sitting in judgment on it. There is only one Lawgiver and Judge,
the one who is able to save and destroy. But you—
who are you to judge your neighbor?*

Slander is such a harsh word. It means *to
make false statements or misrepresentations that
damage a person's reputation.* It is a word that
brings up images of tabloid papers entangled in
litigation with movie stars. We might well claim
that as a Christian—"I NEVER 'slander'." But
actually the phrase James has used is much broader
than the legal definition. The Greek actually
means *any form of speaking against a person*—
and would include even essentially truthful statements made in a harsh or unkind manner. Wow.
That is a different story. We probably all do that
from time to time. The verb tense forbids a "con-
tinuing action" of speaking badly. Do not "continue to speak against one another..." In contem-
porary language—"Stop poor-mouthing. Don't
bad mouth..."

Apparently, James knew that this had become
common among the Christians he was address-
ing—talking badly about one another. He says that
to do so is to stand above the Law. He probably

105

meant the command in Leviticus 19:18 to "love
your neighbor as yourself." As Christians, we can
easily fall into this trap. Sometimes we rationalize
that we are not really judging —but "discerning."
We are not really speaking against that person—
but we are "sharing a concern." Prayer sessions
can easily dissolve into gossip sessions. Brain-
storming can turn into griping. We may even
reason that if we "judge" according to a measure
we are willing to be "judged by"—it is okay. We so
easily fall into judging others—and even judging
ourselves.

James has a strong word for us: *"There is only
one Lawgiver and Judge, the one who is able to
save and destroy. But you—who are you to judge
your neighbor?"* We are not to judge anyone—not
even ourselves! That's right—YOU are your
closest neighbor. You are not allowed to speak
badly even of yourself. You know—the little pity
party you have periodically. Why? Because you
are the creation of God—redeemed at great cost,
and it is the sole place of God to judge. So...

"Hey you..."

"Me?"

"Yes, YOU!"

"Me?"

"Yes—who are YOU—to JUDGE?"

"But I was only beating myself up for all the
mistakes I have made in life..."

"Who are YOU to judge your neighbor, your
family member, another church, or yourself?"

Lord, give me a little pinch today—or even a quick kick in the conscience—if I begin to slander—or speak badly of anyone—even myself. Thank You, Lord. Amen.

The

Lord Willing

James 4:13-17

*Now listen, you who say, "Today or tomorrow we
will go to this or that city, spend a year there,
carry on business and make money." Why, you
do not even know what will happen tomorrow.
What is your life? You are a mist that appears for
a little while and then vanishes. Instead, you ought
to say, "If it is the Lord's will, we will live and do
this or that." As it is, you boast and brag. All such
boasting is evil. Anyone, then, who knows the good
he ought to do and doesn't do it, sins.*

We are certainly a culture of planners. These
days if you have not been to a seminar and made a
"life plan" with a mission statement you obviously
are headed nowhere fast. And losing your
"DayTimer" is tantamount to losing your brain. So
how can James really criticize those who have
direction? Doesn't the Bible say that *"Without
vision—the people perish..."* (Proverbs 29:18).
That is actually where we make a big mistake—we
confuse "vision" (which is from God) with the
"plans of men."

The Word teaches us the difference between
the vision of God and the plans of men. "The Lord
foils the plans of the nations; he thwarts the
purposes of the peoples. But the plans of the Lord
stand firm forever, the purposes of his heart
through all generations" (Psalm 33:10-11).

"Commit to the Lord whatever you do, and

your plans will succeed" (Proverbs 16:3). "In his heart a man plans his course, but the Lord determines his steps" (Proverbs 16:9). "Many are the plans in a man's heart, but it is the Lord's purpose that prevails" (Proverbs 19:21). So are we to live without any plan? Not at all. But our plan must be to pursue God's vision for our lives—not just to dream something up and then ask for God's blessing.

There is a lovely saying that is heard in some parts of the country that flows out of this passage— *"I will be there next Spring... Lord willing..."* That is the key in any plan we make—Give God the flexibility to adjust and even change the course of life. The truth is that our "plans" can often make it more painful for God to use us the way He wants to use us. When we obligate the future—with commitments or financial obligations—we either limit what we expect God to do in our lives or we make it painful to pull away from those plans. This is one of the reasons why many Christian authors teach us to avoid debt.

I have a friend who is fond of saying: "I want to be smack dab in the middle of God's will for my life." There is no more blessed place than in His will. And to know that will—and not be in it—or not be able to get into it because of some obligation—is sin. *"Anyone, then, who knows the good he ought to do and doesn't do it, sins."* That is to say—it clearly falls short of the mark God is aiming for in our lives.

Where are you today? Are you where God wants you to be? Not some dream of where someone else says you should be—but where GOD wants you to be? Our only plan should be the plan to be available when He calls and reveals that to us.

Lord, I realize that this life is passing—like mist that appears for awhile in the eternal picture of things and then is gone. So I want nothing more than to make this life count for You. Show me how to do that—give me vision—Your vision for my life. Amen. ya Baby :)

Unjust Riches

James 5:1-6

Now listen, you rich people, weep and wail because of the misery that is coming upon you. Your wealth has rotted, and moths have eaten your clothes. Your gold and silver are corroded. Their corrosion will testify against you and eat your flesh like fire. You have hoarded wealth in the last days. Look! The wages you failed to pay the workmen who mowed your fields are crying out against you. The cries of the harvesters have reached the ears of the Lord Almighty. You have lived on earth in luxury and self-indulgence. You have fattened yourselves in the day of slaughter. You have condemned and murdered innocent men, who were not opposing you.

James 5:1-6 is one of those Scriptures we will not likely memorize or share as a favorite in a small group. There is nothing warm and fuzzy here! The harsh words of James are reminiscent of the Old Testament prophets and the sharp criticism of injustice (Isaiah 13-21, 23; Ezekiel 25-32). Some scholars give us a little comfort in noting that this does not seem to be directed toward believers but toward pagans because it is not addressed to "brothers." But we would be foolish to turn too quickly from the sting of James' words. We may chuckle and assume this could not be aimed at ourselves unless someone has miraculously paid off our credit cards. But the simple fact is that if we are reading these words in relative western comfort, we are probably among the top percentage of wealthy people in the world.

The sin condemned here is not "being rich." There are four specific sins that occur for the most part only in the trappings of wealth that are condemned. These sins are—*hoarded wealth*—*unpaid wages*—*luxurious self-indulgence*—and the *murder of innocent people*.

Hoarding? We might do well occasionally to ask how much is enough. You don't have to be Donald Trump to find yourself accumulating more stuff than you really need. Is there some stuff that could be given to the poor?

The wages of workers? Sadly there are occasions when employers—even Christians—even church employers fail to pay a fair wage or try to get by without a paying what is due. Sometimes what is technically legal—is not right or fair or just. Are you in business—or management? Pay fairly all of every wage.

How about luxurious self-indulgence? That probably happens any time we spend beyond bare necessity or splurge on a brand name. It is difficult not to buy beyond the generic brand—but it is certainly something we can watch and even balance in special giving.

Hopefully we have not participated in the killing of innocents—especially since James was probably referring to Christian martyrs. But we may give thought to whether we have responsibility for damage or death that comes to people through a corporation we support or a system from which we benefit. Do we have any social responsibility for a company we do business with—that chooses to negotiate legal damages rather than recall a product that is dangerous? Do we have a responsibility if our health care system experiments with fetal tissue? In the wealth of our highly technical culture—the answers will become more and more difficult.

How will we make it? Only with the grace of God.

Lord, is there something You want me to change? Have I been unfair? Is there a part of my life-style that I could change? Could I live more simply? Is there something more that You would like for me to give? Even things, perhaps, that I just don't need anymore? Lord, show me how to be connected in ways that give life—always life. Give me the grace to carefully manage the wealth You have entrusted to me. Amen.

Patience

James 5:7-11

Be patient, then, brothers, until the Lord's coming.
See how the farmer waits for the land to yield its
valuable crop and how patient he is for the au-
tumn and spring rains. You too, be patient and
stand firm, because the Lord's coming is near.
Don't grumble against each other, brothers, or you
will be judged. The Judge is standing at the door!
Brothers, as an example of patience in the face of
suffering, take the prophets who spoke in the name
of the Lord. As you know, we consider blessed
those who have persevered. You have heard of Job's
perseverance and have seen what the Lord finally
brought about. The Lord is full of compassion and
mercy.

James is not talking about the "general patience" that we need waiting at a stoplight or
dealing with our children. Persecution was intense
in the early decades of the church. Suffering was
real. Sticking with the faith had become costly.
James has just finished a blistering condemnation
of the sins committed by the unjust rich, but that
doesn't really help if there is a famine and you
have lost your business connections due to your
faith.

Is there any encouragement for those who are
suffering? The Lord is coming back. But when will
that relief come? We must be patient—says
James—like the farmer who knows that the crop

will come in the Spring. If the season is dry—the farmer will face some anxious times—but the crop is coming to be sure. We need patience like the prophets of old—who put everything on the line to announce a judgement—and even a redemption—that they would never see with their own eyes. Or think about Moses, whose entire life work was spent getting people to a promised land that he did not enter! Or the patience of Job who finally saw the blessing of God restored after dealing with incredible losses.

Perhaps even more comforting is the balance in this passage. On the one hand—"the Judge is standing at the door!" On the other hand "The Lord is full of compassion and mercy." He is coming. There will be justice. There will also be mercy and compassion. God is good in all those departments. It may be we just miss that eternal perspective—when we get frustrated by job situations and inconveniences—when we struggle over church disputes or differences of doctrine—when we are hurting—we miss what is lasting.

In the big picture—very few things here will matter when the Lord comes back. The only things that really matter are relationships. Your relationship with God—with people and yourself. That focus goes a long way toward the kind of patience James is talking about. But when will the return be? You will hear all sorts of predictions especially as the beginning of a new millennium approaches. But the message of James is consistent with the rest of the Bible. Be patient. Be ready. The judge is at the door. The Lord is full of compassion and mercy. Where does this patience come from?

From the One who is at the door—full of compassion and mercy.

Lord, help me to live this day for You. Give me some perspective to live this day as though it may be my last. Let me focus on the things that count—things that are eternal. Amen.

Truth

James 5:12

Above all, my brothers, do not swear—not by heaven or by earth or by anything else. Let your "Yes" be yes, and your "No," no, or you will be condemned.

James begins by saying—"Above all." That must mean that what follows is really—REALLY—important, even though it sounds rather simple. James is actually quoting Jesus as recorded in Matthew 5:34-37: *"But I tell you, Do not swear at all: either by heaven, for it is God's throne; or by the earth, for it is his footstool; or by Jerusalem, for it is the city of the Great King, And do not swear by your head, for you cannot make even one hair white or black. Simply let your 'Yes' be 'Yes,' and your 'No,' 'No'; anything beyond this comes from the evil one."*

Jewish tradition in the first century had developed a sophisticated system for making oaths and judging whether a particular oath was binding over another oath or commitment. An oath made "to the Lord"—was considered payable as if owed to God. Various oaths were made "by" heaven—or earth—or Jerusalem and on and on. These were judged in a complicated hierarchy of rabbinical rulings based on how they related to the Lord and the order of creation. One oath might supersede and nullify another based on these rulings. An entire tract of the mishnah was devoted to this hair splitting process!

Knowledge of these rules allowed one to make business commitments and then not be held accountable. It sounds ridiculous and we might find it humorous—until we consider the way that our own modern culture carefully crafts legal language that "admits no culpability" and "surrenders no responsibility." Legal doublespeak is perhaps surpassed only by the skill of the highly compensated "spin doctors" who shape public image and debate in political arena.

It is clear—that we are broken humans—in our sinful state—who have a terrible time with honesty whether in the first century or the twentieth. Our gift of language ought to set us above the animals—but in our sin nature we use careful wordcraft to deceive—to say what we do not mean—or to provide for a way to escape our commitments. So to our world of "qualified statement" and careful caveats—James hits us between the dotted *i's* with the words of Jesus: *"Let your "Yes" be yes, and your "No," no"*—even adding this consequence—"or you will be condemned."

Why so strong a statement? Perhaps it is because dishonesty in our words reveals a deeper fundamental problem in our relationship with God. Consider 1 John 1:6: *"If we claim to have fellowship with Him yet walk in the darkness, we lie and do not live by the truth."* Failure to tell the truth is a fruit of something other than God's Spirit. Jesus made it clear. He did not come to share truth—or extol truth—or suggest truth. Jesus said: *I AM the truth*. If the truth lives within us—that should be reflected in what comes out of us. No wonder

James cautions—above all—*let your Yes be Yes and your No be No.*

So. How are you doing in the truth department? As you think about your day today—will you be a man or woman of your word? Will you hedge the truth—or doctor the spin? Can those around you count on the Truth of Jesus Who lives in you?

Lord, You are the TRUTH. Come and live in me anew—speak through me—flow through me. Let my mouth honor You with integrity. Give me courage to speak plainly. I pray that those around me may count on what I say—because they see You in me. Amen.

Pray

James 5:13-16

Is any one of you in trouble? He should pray. Is anyone happy? Let him sing songs of praise. Is any one of you sick? He should call the elders of the church to pray over him and anoint him with oil in the name of the Lord. And the prayer offered in faith will make the sick person well; the Lord will raise him up. If he has sinned, he will be forgiven. Therefore confess your sins to each other and pray for each other so that you may be healed. The prayer of a righteous man is powerful and effective.

The Christian life is one of balance. When in trouble—(lit. *afflicted*)—we *pray* or make supplication. When happy—in times of goodness, blessing and cheer—we *sing*. The word *sing* means to *vibrate like a string played by a bow.* Our rejoicing is the resonance of God's Spirit playing the strings of our soul. But if we are sick— we should call. Call not only to God because that is supplication—but call on the healing community. God heals through the touch of His hands— the body of Christ.

From time to time someone will ask—"Who are these 'Elders'?" Of course they may be those who hold an office of approved or elected leadership. But I often say—"They are the ones you call on to pray when you are sick..." They are obvious in most communities of faith. They are people of fervent powerful, faith-filled prayer—whether recognized by official title or not. They are the prayer warriors who stand ready to battle against the enemy. Satan trembles when they quietly fold their hands and look heavenward.

Why anoint with oil? Three reasons. First, the Bible says to do so—Second, the Bible says to do so—Third, the Bible says to do so. There is no "magic" in the oil, but it is a symbol of the presence and power of the Holy Spirit. The word *Christ* means—*anointed one.* So oil is a powerful symbol of the presence of Christ and the faith of the community. Oil was also a form of medicine in the ancient world. So James was additionally instructing us to add the best medical care possible to our prayers of faith. This is medical "anointing" "in the name of the Lord." "And the prayer offered in faith will make the sick person well; the Lord will raise him up." The Greek word *to raise* is used in two ways in the New Testament—*to be raised up from sickness*—and also *to be raised from the dead.* Both of these are part of the healing provided in Jesus. The ultimate healing we seek is in the resurrection. The prayer offered in faith WILL be answered even if not in our desired time. God heals—but His greatest concern is eternal.

Sometimes the eternal dimension of healing requires something deeper than any physical medicine can treat. *"If he has sinned, he will be forgiven. Therefore confess your sins to each other and pray for each other so that you may be healed. The prayer of a righteous man is powerful and effective."* It is not that God punishes sin with sickness—but sometimes we are just "sin sick". Our misery has to do with our fundamental brokenness. Until we confess that we are powerless to be whole without Him, we will never find peace. To _confess_ means to _agree with_. We must agree with God that we need Him and we are broken without Him. Confessing—agreeing with God—in the presence of a trusted member of the community of faith is to discover that we do not fight the battles alone. Confession requires that we take off the mask of self-reliance and begin to get better. The prayer of a "righteous person" is simply the prayer of a confessed person. That prayer— the one that has nothing to hide—that knows how desperately we need God—that righteous prayer— is powerful and effective.

Lord, give me balance. Teach me to sing.
Play me like a violin with the bow of Your Spirit.
In my times of affliction, draw me near in prayers
of faith to You and to my healing community of
faith. I agree with You—that I am lost without
You. And I praise You that You have pursued a
love relationship with me in the person of Jesus.
Amen.

Elijah

James 5:17-18

Elijah was a man just like us. He prayed earnestly that it would not rain, and it did not rain on the land for three and a half years. Again he prayed, and the heavens gave rain, and the earth produced its crops.

Elijah was a man just like us. Oh, really? Have you read the story lately? Here was a guy who had an anointing to confront false prophets by the hundreds—to mock them—and then to call down fire from heaven just to make the point. He was no ordinary preacher. Is this a "man just like us"? Perhaps the point is that in spite of the flashy appearance and special effects of Elijah's ministry (1 Kings 17-19), he was above all a man of prayer (1 Kings 18:42).

For all the flash, we have to realize that nothing happened for Elijah except out of a surrendered relationship before the Lord. The really human part of Elijah comes out at Mount Horeb—not Mount Carmel. Elijah had perhaps the greatest day of preaching in history. He had won the debate with the false prophets, and God had come through with fire. But then Elijah runs away from that victory and huddles under a broom tree in what might be described as a deep depression. It is only when the Lord ministers to Him and reveals power to him in the form of the whirlwind—that Elijah is strengthened to return to the call of the

Lord. Maybe Elijah *is* a man just like us.

The life of prayer is about earnest supplication—but it also is about really struggling with the Lord and being drained after the victories. The life of prayer is about times when the Lord ministers to us under the broom trees where we hide. The life of prayer is about rare and awesome moments when the wind of His Spirit passes by and restores us to His work.

How is your prayer life? Prayer is not just about praying and getting answers. Prayer is a relationship with God—of listening—hearing—obeying—being drained—being restored—hearing the wind—returning for more.

Lord, I want to hear the wind. Lift me to new places. Teach me how to pray the prayer of faith. Thank You for seeking me out under my broom trees—and restoring me for prayer and service. Now let me soar with You. Amen.

Bring Home the Wounded

James 5:19-20

My brothers, if one of you should wander from the truth and someone should bring him back, remember this: Whoever turns a sinner from the error of his way will save him from death and cover over a multitude of sins.

This is the last of our reading. The book of James ends rather uneventfully. No farewell. No personal greetings. No benediction. But someone once advised that we should pay careful attention to the "things said last"—because they are often the things that come from the heart.

Remember—James was speaking in a time of persecution. Some had fallen away from their new found faith. Some had wandered. Suddenly—in these closing comments—James is not talking about the taming of the tongue or the philosophy of faith versus works. The heart of James is to address things that are eternal.

What James suggests probably would not sit well in our modern culture of tolerance. We are often taught today that faith is important and "any faith will do." James suggests that much more is at stake. Today, people talk of having discovered things "spiritual"—but they mean a whole variety of pagan religious thoughts that have nothing to do with Scriptural Christianity. The truth is that there are more places than ever to "wander." James—? What are we to do? He says: *Someone should bring them back.* Is it really too intrusive to gently question a friend or family member who wanders—when there is so much at stake? Paul advised in Galatians 6:1 that when a brother or sister is caught—stuck in sin—we are to restore them gently. The word Paul uses means *medically to put a dislocated joint back into a socket.* That process is painful—but when gently applied—the outcome is nothing but good. Jesus taught the same thing in His parables of the lost coin and the lost sheep (Luke 15). When a soul has wandered—or just slipped away like a coin—the heart of God seeks and searches until that wandering soul is restored.

Can you think of any wanderers today? Maybe a family member or friend—? Is there someone that you have missed lately at church or in class? Sometimes just a gentle invitation to come back is all that is needed.

Lord, forgive me for failing to notice those who have wandered. Give me Your seeking, searching heart. Give me also the grace to gently restore those who have gotten stuck somewhere. In Jesus' name. Amen.

Faith that Works

So what is a faith that works? Can we really find a faith that will not break down? Is there a faith that actually works in this age? The answer from James, the brother of Jesus, is a resounding: YES!

A faith that works is found in complete surrender to Jesus. In this faith, we are constantly reminded of who we are—and Whose we are. It is a faith that gives us identity and then sends us out, scattered into the world, to be salt and light. It is a faith that carries us through trial and fills us with joy. It is not an easy faith but it is a faith that perseveres and is strengthened by hard times.

Faith that works has an eternal perspective. It is a faith that casts the whole weight of life, in complete trust, upon the Lord Jesus. It is a faith that steps out from the world, without wavering, into the Kingdom of God. It is a faith that recognizes exactly where eternal riches lie and that the high position in Christ may be completely different from that defined by the world.

This faith goes to work reforming the priorities of life. It is a faith that causes us to see what is really important so that we reach for a crown that is eternal and pass by that which is fading. It is a faith refined in the times of temptation. This faith gives us eyes to see the hand of God in every good gift and causes us to offer ourselves back to God.

There is no ducking or dodging around this faith that works. We will be refined! This faith will not abide with sin. The Word of God goes to work in us, by faith, refining our actions and defining our responses. In this faith, we suddenly discover what real "religion" is all about—helping the least among us.

Such faith goes to work fast on the relationships of life. Relationships are restored but not just with the people close to us. We learn to live out a faith that has no favorites and respects all persons. Rich and poor are redefined. We discover a faith that is alive and responsive to needs around us. Grace and mercy are manifest in marvelous ways.

It is in the walk of life, that this faith makes a powerful impact. Faith is completed when belief becomes action. Labels are thrown away! We hear with understanding what it means live out the love of God as we love people. With every word and deed, we teach the Gospel of Christ.

Faith that works is able to trust God even to transform the untamed animal of the tongue! By this powerful faith, surrendered to Him, God transforms our words and brings fresh water where once there was brine! The wretched sin of gossip really can be overcome. Fighting can be set aside. Our mouth can become a fresh spring of water that blesses God and the people around us.

We are called away from the world by a faith that works. So enticing is this relationship with

God that we submit in love to our heavenly Father. Faith that works is victorious! Faith that works will resist the devil who then must flee from us! The ways of the world are set aside. Slander is no more. Unjust gain is not even a consideration. We trust God for tomorrow and seek His future with joy!

Most of all, faith that works places us in a relationship with God through our Lord, Jesus. With our trust wholly in Him, and not in any work of our flesh, we patiently await His return for us. In our waiting, we love Him. We tell His truth as people of integrity. We pray for His people to be whole. We feel the wind of His Spirit upon our faces. We restore those who are wounded.

James presents us with a choice. We can settle for a flimsy faith that will fold with the first tough battle— an easy beliefism that will not transform a thing. Or, we can wholly surrender in faith to the Lord Jesus Christ, and watch as that faith goes to work transforming us. Nothing is quite as exhilarating.

Lord, Jesus, give us faith that works. Amen.

About the Author

Dr. Jeffrey D. Hoy is founder and Senior Pastor of Faith Fellowship Church in Melbourne, Florida. Faith Fellowship is one of the fastest growing Evangelical Free Churches in the country. Dr. Hoy is a graduate of the Candler School of Theology at Emory University in Atlanta, Georgia and has pastored churches in Florida for the past 15 years. You can reach Dr. Hoy by writing to Faith Fellowship Church, P.O. Box 410646 Melbourne, Florida 32941-0646. His E-mail address is jeffhoy@xc.com. His web page address is http://www.ff-efca.org/ and his phone number is 407-259-7200.

Internet Ministry

Dr. Hoy is author of the popular E-mail devotional called *Words of Faith* which reaches thousands of readers in over a dozen countries around the world. *Words of Faith* gives busy people who regularly use E-mail a quiet moment to reflect in the Word of God. It is also distributed by missionaries and parachurches as a way of enriching Christian workers. Many individuals have received God's Grace through these devotions and your life can be touched as well. As one reader puts it, "I am so excited to read your devotional each day. It is an awesome reminder that God has us in the palm of His hand and truly knows what we need before we ask or think it." To subscribe to *Words of Faith*, send E-mail to jeffhoy@xc.com.

Ordering Information

To order additional copies of this book, send a check or money order to Halyard Press, Inc., P.O. Box 410308 Melbourne, FL 32941-0308. The price per book is $9.95. Order 10 or more copies at $6.95 each. Florida residents add 6 percent sales tax. Please add the following amount for shipping and handling: one or two books add $3.00; three to nine books add $3 plus $1 per quantity over two; ten books or more books add 5 percent of the total book price.